S0-DZC-645

Pterodactylus
This flying reptile
lived at the same time
as the dinosaurs.

Diplodocus
Padded heels softened
this huge plant-eater's
thundering footsteps.

Compsognathus
This chicken-sized
dinosaur ate lizards
and insects.

Brachiosaurus's long neck was balanced by a long tail.

Brachiosaurus
At about 60 tons,
this dinosaur was
one of the heaviest.

Ornithosuchus
This dinosaur walked
on all fours, but ran
on its two back legs.

Suchomimus
Bones of this meat-
eater were first found
in Africa in 1998.

Archaeopteryx
This birdlike creature lived at the same time as the dinosaurs.

Barosaurus
At over 80 ft (24 m) long, this was one of the biggest dinosaurs.

Coelophysis
This dinosaur may have been a cannibal.

Some dinosaurs fed on frogs.

nt life
ny dinosaurs only
plants.

Last dinosaurs

Among the last dinosaurs to live on
Earth were the fiercest meat-eaters,
including Tyrannosaurus rex. They
roamed the landscape, in which flow-
ering plants and trees grew.
Dinosaurs became extinct (died
out) about 65 million years ago.

Corythosaurus
This large, duck-billed
dinosaur had a high,
narrow crest on its head.

Caudipteryx
A small, birdlike
dinosaur, Caudipteryx
was covered in feathers.

Edmontonia
This flat-headed
dinosaur had a ducklike
beak and fed on plants.

1

2

3

4

5

7

6

9

8

10

11

12

13

14

16

17

15

19

18

20

21

22

23

25

26

27

28

29

30

31

32

33

34

35

36

37

39

40

Iguanodon

This dinosaur may have used its bony beak to nip leaves off plants.

Deinonychus

They hunted in packs, searching for dinosaurs and animals.

Maiasaura mothers laid their eggs in mounds.

Dinosaur nest

Nests of Maiasaura eggs and babies have been discovered in Montana.

Early dinosaurs

Dinosaurs roamed the Earth millions of years ago, long before humans existed. The earliest dinosaurs were mostly nimble meat-eaters. Later, herds of giant plant-eating dinosaurs appeared. The landscape was filled with forests of conifers (trees with needles and cones) and ferns covered the ground.

Heterodontosaurus
This small but fast-moving dinosaur was about 3 ft (1 m) long.

Anchisaurus
This small, light dinosaur had very strong thumb claws.

Crocodiles ate river animals and dead dinosaurs

Dimorphodon
A flying reptile that had a wingspan of 4.5 ft (1.4 m).

25

Barosaurus
Its whiplike tail may have been used to lash out at enemies.

Herrerasaurus
The Herrerasaurus was a meat-eater and a very agile hunter.

Stegosaurus had two rows of plates on its back.

Stegosaurus
A large, slow-moving dinosaur, Stegosaurus ate low-level plants.

Ferns
Small plant-eating dinosaurs ate ferns as well as other ground plants.

Flying reptiles and the first birds began to appear

Allosaurus
This fierce, fat-necked meat-eater preyed on other dinosaurs.

Dilophosaurus
This fierce hunter had two large crests on its head.